Gerngross · Puchta · Becker
PLAYWAY 4

PUPIL'S BOOK

	Starter **School is cool** 2
	Unit 1 **Pets and other animals** 4
	Unit 2 **In town** 10
	Unit 3 **Birthdays** 16
	Unit 4 **Shopping** 22
	Unit 5 **Free time** 28
	Unit 6 **Feelings** 34

	Unit 7 **Time** 40
	Unit 8 **At home** 46
	Unit 9 **Food and drink** 52
Special days	**Halloween** 58
	Christmas around the world 59
	Valentine's Day 60
	Pancake Day 61
	Word list **English – German** 62

Starter: School is cool

★ **1** 2/3 Listen and point. Test your partner. Sing the song.

Oh, what a lovely morning

You're in bed,
and you wake up.
You check your watch.
It's time to get up!

Oh, what a lovely morning,
it's time to go to school.
Oh, what a lovely morning,
school is so cool!

Wash your face,
put on your clothes.
Have a glass of milk.
Take your bag and off you go!

Oh, what a lovely morning,
it's time to go to school.
Oh, what a lovely morning,
school is so cool!

★ **2** 5 Listen. Then change the dialogue and act it out.

Grace: Harry?
Harry: Yes, Grace?
Grace: I've got a new computer game.
Harry: Great.
Grace: Can you come to my house?
Harry: OK. When?
Grace: At three.
Harry: OK.
Grace: Great! Bye.
Harry: Bye.

Clever Joe

⭐ **3** 📺 **Watch the story.** 🔊 6 **Listen and read.**

1  Pets and other animals

⭐ **1** 🎵 7 **Listen and point. Then test your partner.**

1. hamster
2. cat
3. spider
4. fish
5. dog
6. guinea pig
7. pony
8. rabbit
9. tortoise
10. mouse
11. snake
12. budgie

⭐ **2 Play the memory game.**

Pinky, the elephant

★ 3 Watch the story. Listen and read.

1 Pets and other animals

4 Look and read.

5 Listen and read.

LOOK!
He/She's got = He/She has got
I/We/They've got = I/We/They have got

Hi, we're Laura and Jim. We've got a dog. It's two years old.

Hello, I'm Ann. I've got a guinea pig. It's eleven months old.

Hi, I'm David. I've got a budgie. It's three years old.

Hi, we're Emily and Charlotte. We've got a pony. It's five years old.

6 Remember and speak.

What about Ann?

What about Emily and Charlotte?

She's got a …
It's … old.

They've got a …
It's … old.

7 Read the text. Find the correct picture.

Lara's horse is white, brown and black.
It's six years old.

It's picture number …

8 Play the guessing game.

The horse is …   It's picture number …

My text

9 Read. Write your own text.

My text

I haven't got a pet.
My grandma has got a budgie.
It's yellow and green.

10 Read. Write your own text.

My text

I've got a cat. My cat's name is Snuggles. He's white and grey. I love my cat. He sleeps in my bed. My little sister has got two rabbits. They are brown and white. They like carrots and broccoli.

1 Pets and other animals

⭐ **11** 🎧 11/12 **Listen. Sing the song.**

Mice, mice, mice

Mice, mice, mice,
I like their little ears.

Mice, mice, mice,
I like their little feet.

Mice, mice, mice,
I like their little teeth.
Yes, little mice are really nice!

My mum hates mice,
my dad hates mice,
but I think mice are really nice.

I give them cheese,
I give them rice.
Yes, mice are really nice!

⭐ **12** **Work with a partner. What animal is it?**

I think number 1 is a …

I think so too. /
I don't think so.
Number 1 is a …

Have you got a pet?

★ 13 🔊 13 **Listen and read.**

★ 14 Ask five classmates. Make notes.

Name	Animal	Colour	How old?
Natalie	hamster	brown	3 years
David	—	—	—

★★ 15 Tell the class.

Natalie has got a hamster.
It's brown.
It's three years old.
David hasn't got a pet.

Ethan and Katie have got a …
It's …

KV 4

2   In town

★ **1** 🔊 14 Listen and point. Then test your partner.

1. zoo
2. hospital
3. museum
4. cinema
5. supermarket
6. library
7. post office
8. swimming pool
9. sweet shop
10. restaurant
11. playground
12. bus stop
13. train station

★ **2** Play the memory game.

What's number 5?
Yes.
I think it's the supermarket.

3 Listen and point.

Turn left.

Go straight on.

Turn right.

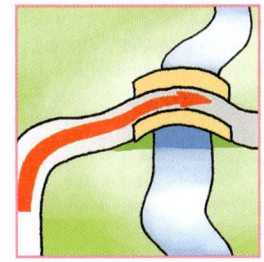
Go across the bridge.

4 Listen. Then act out the dialogues.

Dialogue 1:

Tourist: Excuse me, please. Where's the cinema?
Woman: It's on Market Street.
Tourist: Where's that?
Woman: Go straight on. Then turn right at the park.
Tourist: Thank you.

Dialogue 2:

Tourist: Excuse me, where's the supermarket?
Man: OK. Turn left here. Then go across the bridge. You can see the supermarket from the bridge.
Tourist: Thank you very much.
Man: That's OK.

Dialogue 3:

Tourist: Excuse me, please.
Woman: Yes?
Tourist: Where's the zoo?
Woman: Look, there's a bus stop over there.
Tourist: A bus stop?
Woman: Yes, bus 18 takes you to the zoo.
Tourist: Thank you.

2  In town

★ 5 18-20 **Listen. Do the chant.**

Where's the park?

Where's the park? Where's the park?
That's easy. That's easy.
Turn left, turn left,
go straight across the bridge,
turn right, turn right.
Thanks a lot.
All right.
All right.

 6 **Work in pairs. Speak.**

Excuse me, please. Where's the hospital?

Go …

⭐ **7** Look and read. Say which sentences are *True* or *False*.

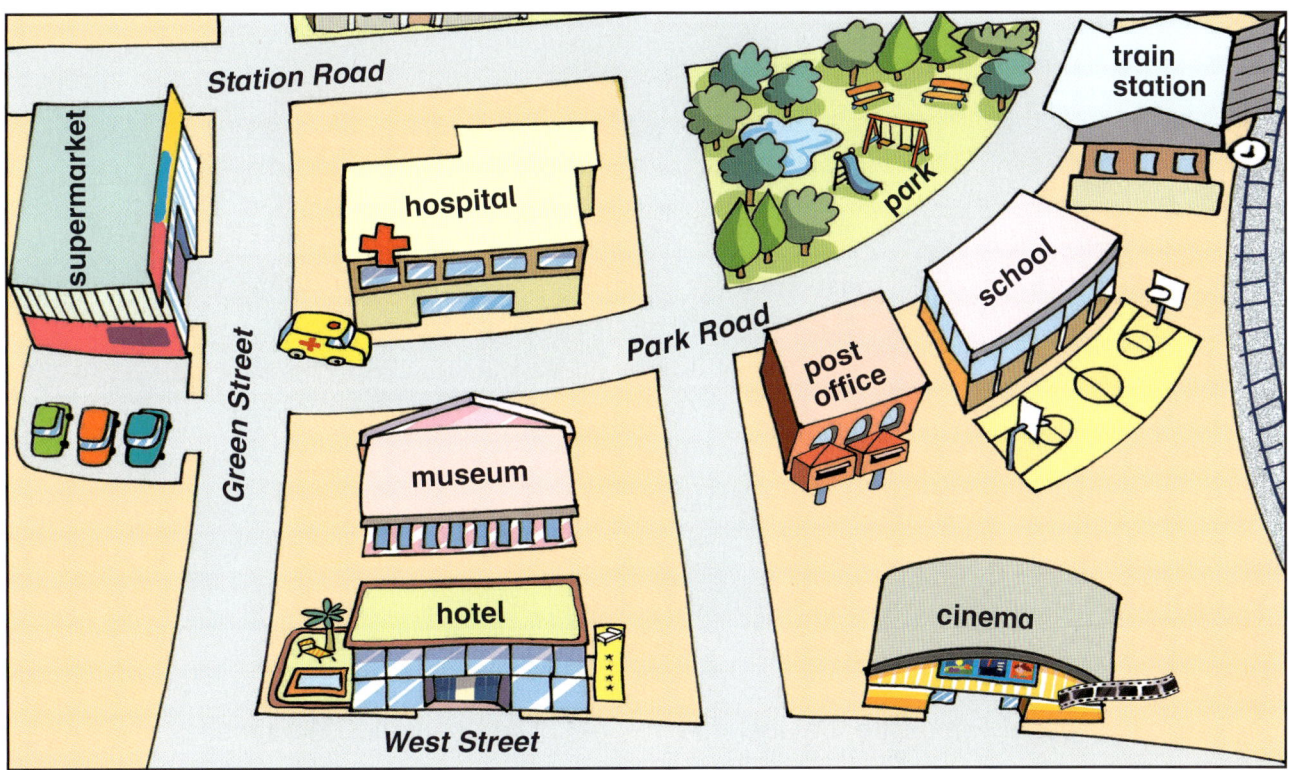

1. The post office is on Green Street.
2. The school is next to the post office.
3. The hospital is opposite the museum.
4. The school is opposite the park.
5. The cinema is next to the hospital.
6. The supermarket is on Green Street.
7. The train station is opposite the museum.
8. The hotel is on Park Road.
9. The supermarket is opposite the school.
10. The hospital is on Park Road.

Number 1 is false.

⭐ **8** Correct the wrong sentences from **7**.

The post office is on Park Road.
...

2  In town

9 Look at the picture and read the texts. Say which text is true.

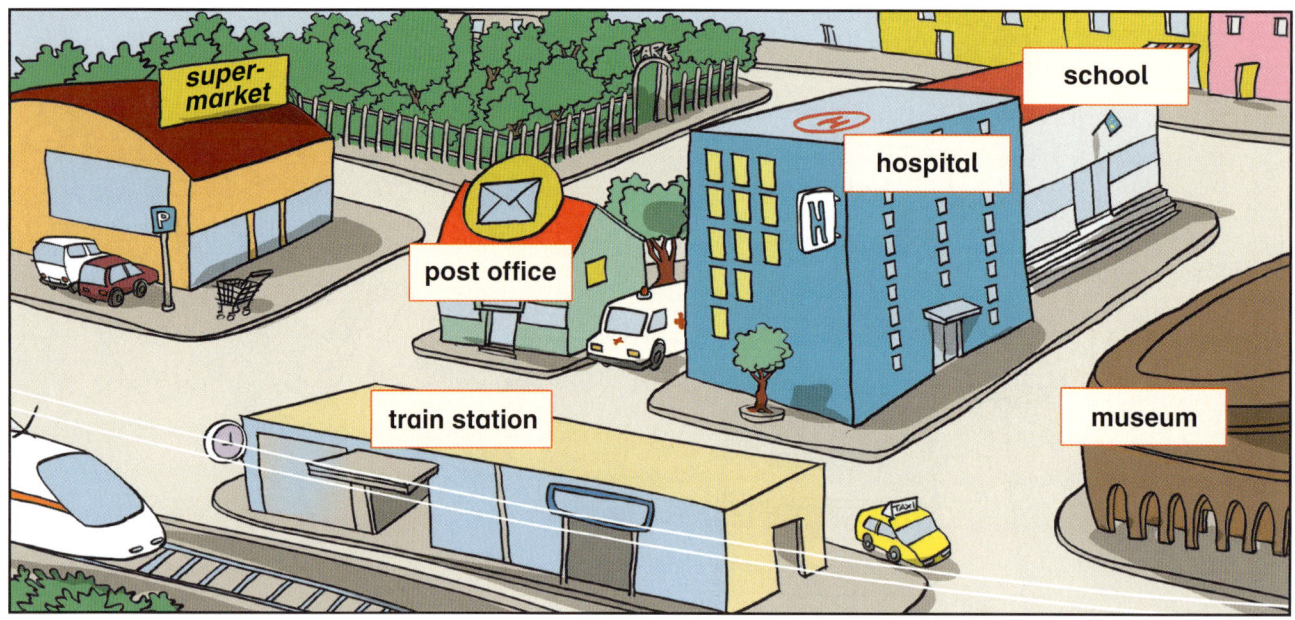

1
The train station is opposite the hospital and the post office. The park is opposite the supermarket. The school is next to the museum.

2
The post office is opposite the supermarket. The school is next to the hospital. The train station is opposite the hospital and the post office.

My text

10 Read. Write your own text.

> My text
> My house is on King's Street.
> It's opposite the playground.

11 Read. Write your own text.

> My text
> Turn right at the school and go straight on. Then turn left at the library.
> Go straight on and turn right at the supermarket. Then go straight on across the bridge. My house is on the left. It's number 10.

14

Mia and Mike in London

12 Look at the photos. Guess the answers. Then watch and check.

Which picture shows …
- Big Ben?
- the London Eye?
- Tower Bridge?
- Buckingham Palace?

Number 1 is …

A group project: Sightseeing in London

Practise role plays in groups.

Look over there! That's …	Wow. It looks great / very nice.
Do you know what that is?	Yes, I think it's … / I have no idea.
Let's go and see …	Yes, good idea. / No, let's go …

3 Birthdays

⭐ 1 🎧 24-26 **Listen. Do the chant.**

LOOK!
My birthday's in May. = My birthday is in May.

My birthday

My birthday's not in January,
in February or March.
My birthday's not in April,
in May or in June.

It isn't in July, in August
or September.

It isn't in October
or even in November.

Remember, remember,
my birthday's in December.

⭐ 2 🎧 27 **Listen. Then play a guessing game.**

Sandra, is your birthday in summer? — No, it isn't.
Is it in autumn? — Yes, it is.
Is it in September? — No, it isn't.
Is it in October? — Yes, it is.

Daisy's birthday

3 Watch the story and say words you remember. Finish the sentences.

1. I want a lovely present for my daughter. What …?

2. This one? I want …

3. Blow out the candles and …

4. What is it, Dad? I can't tell you. It's …

4   29 **Listen and read.**

Aaron:	Good morning.
Shop assistant:	Good morning.
Aaron:	It's my friend's birthday tomorrow. I want that T-shirt, please.
Shop assistant:	This one?
Aaron:	Yes.
Shop assistant:	Here you are.
Aaron:	Thank you.

5 **Do a role play.**

17

3 Birthdays

★ 6  32 **Listen and read. Match the invitations to the parties.**

1
Come to my party on Saturday.
Bring your bike, bring your ball, and much more.
Come at four!

2
Come to my party on Sunday.
Are you scared of monsters?
Are you scared of rats?
Are you scared of snakes?
Or are you scared of bats?
See you then at two.
My house is near the zoo.

3
My party's on Friday.
Bring some oranges, bring some kiwis, bring bananas, apples and pears.
Meet me at my door right at four.

4
Please come to my party on Saturday.
Meet me by the sea at three.
Let's have some fun in the sun!

beach party    monster party    sports party    fruit party

Invitation number 1 is for the beach party.

I don't think so. It's for the …

7 Look at **6**. Which party are they going to? When is it?

Cathy

James

Violet

Jonas

Cathy is going to the … party. It's on … at …

8 Read the emails. Find the missing information (time, day of the week or address).

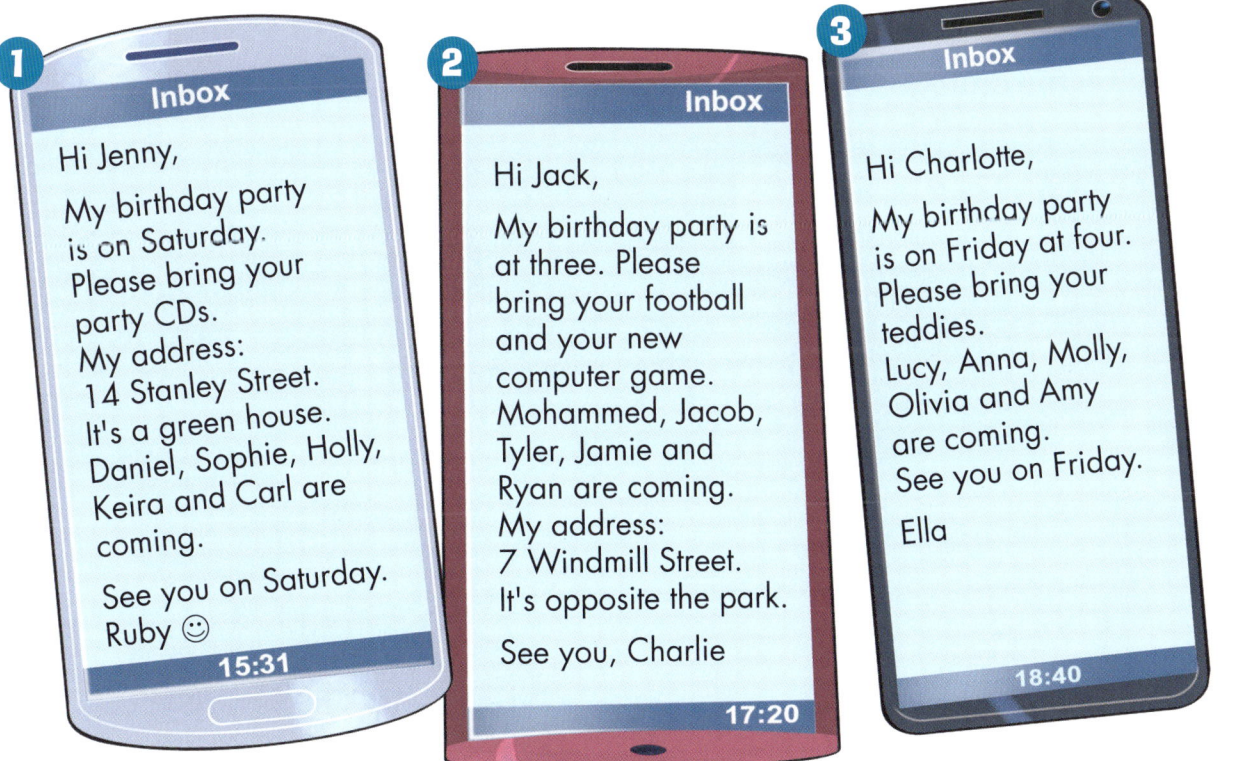

1 Inbox

Hi Jenny,

My birthday party is on Saturday. Please bring your party CDs.
My address: 14 Stanley Street. It's a green house.
Daniel, Sophie, Holly, Keira and Carl are coming.

See you on Saturday.
Ruby ☺

15:31

2 Inbox

Hi Jack,

My birthday party is at three. Please bring your football and your new computer game.
Mohammed, Jacob, Tyler, Jamie and Ryan are coming.
My address: 7 Windmill Street. It's opposite the park.

See you, Charlie

17:20

3 Inbox

Hi Charlotte,

My birthday party is on Friday at four. Please bring your teddies.
Lucy, Anna, Molly, Olivia and Amy are coming.
See you on Friday.

Ella

18:40

KV 10   19

3 Birthdays

⭐ **9** 🎵 33 **Listen and read.**

⭐ **10 Change the dialogue and act it out.**

Birthday presents

11 🎧 35 **Listen and point.**

ball   necklace   CD   car   ring
bike   T-shirt   book   pencil case   watch
skateboard   poster   kite   trainers   coloured pencils

12 🎧 36 **Listen and read the poem.**

My birthday presents

A book, a ball, CDs, a car,
a birthday cake, a golden star.
A camera, a happy cow,
that's what's on my table now.

13 **Write your own poem.**

4 Shopping

★ **1** 🎧 37 Listen and point. Then test your partner.

- 10 ten
- 20 twenty
- 30 thirty
- 40 forty
- 50 fifty
- 60 sixty
- 70 seventy
- 80 eighty
- 90 ninety
- 100 a hundred

★ **2** Play the memory game.

How much are the green shoes?

They're …

⭐ **3** 🎧 38/39 **Listen. Sing the song.**

A hundred big black ravens

A hundred big black ravens
are flying after you.
They want to steal your piggy bank.
So this is what you do:

You pull a face,
you shake your fist,
you shout, 'No way!'
and ten fly away.

Ninety …
Seventy …
Fifty …
Thirty …
Ten …

Eighty …
Sixty …
Forty …
Twenty …

⭐ **4** 🎧 40 **Listen and point.**

LOOK! 100p = £1

British money

5p	10p	20p	50p	£1	£2
five pence	ten pence	twenty pence	fifty pence	one pound	two pounds

£5	£10	£20	£50
five pounds	ten pounds	twenty pounds	fifty pounds

4 Shopping

⭐ **5** 🔊 41 **Listen and point.**

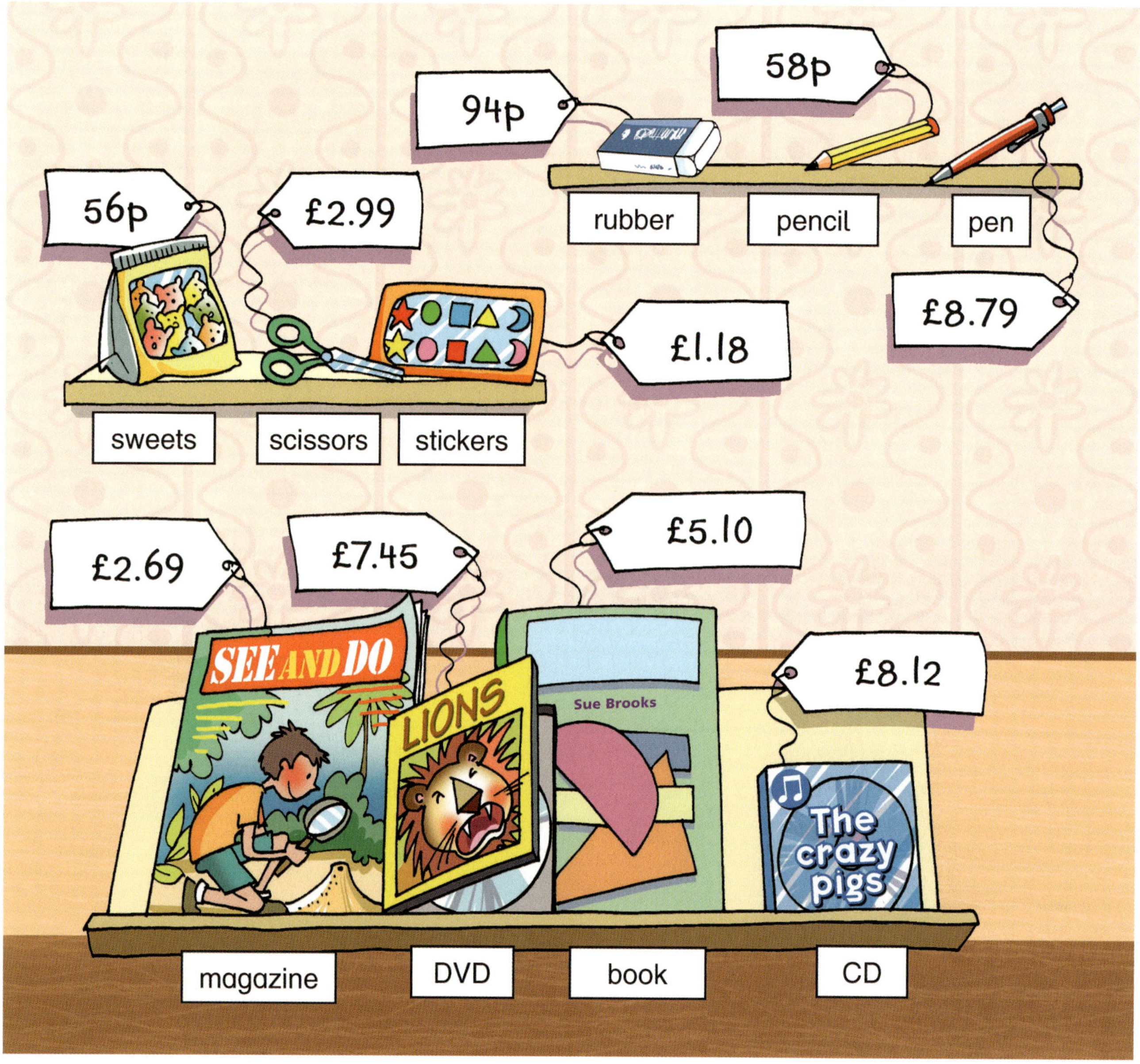

⭐ **6 Look at number 5. Ask and answer.**

How much is the magazine?

It's …

LOOK!
How much **is** the book? – It**'s** …
How much **are** the sweet**s**? – They**'re** …

4

7   **Listen and read. Change and act out.**

Leo & Stella:	Good morning.
Shopkeeper:	Good morning.
Stella:	How much is that **magazine**?
Shopkeeper:	It's **£2.69**.
Leo:	How much **are the sweets**?
Shopkeeper:	They're **56 p**.
Stella:	The sweets and the magazine, please.
Shopkeeper:	That's **£3.25**.
Stella:	Here you are.
Shopkeeper:	Thank you.
Leo & Stella:	Goodbye.
Shopkeeper:	Bye.

Thank you.

Here you are.

8 **Read. Write your own text.**

My text

I often go shopping with my mum. The supermarket is on White Street.

9 **Read. Write your own text.**

My text

I often go shopping with my dad. We go to a supermarket or a farmer's market. We buy apples, potatoes, cheese, tomatoes, milk and flowers.

KV 12 KV 13 S. 19 25

4 Shopping

Going shopping

10 Watch the story and say words you remember. Finish the sentences.

11  Listen and read.

Oscar:	Dad, there's no food in the house.
Clara:	Can you go shopping?
Dad:	Sorry, I'm busy.
Oscar:	Please, Dad.
Dad:	OK. Let's make a shopping list.
Oscar:	Cheese, eggs and milk.
Clara:	Apples, carrots and oranges.
Dad:	OK. Are you coming with me?
Oscar & Clara:	Sorry, Dad. We're going to the park.

12 Do a role play.

What do you buy?

13 Do interviews in class. Make notes.

bread fish a hot dog chewing gum fruit ice cream

sweets a T-shirt milk CDs chocolate a magazine

Do you often go shopping?
What do you buy?

Yes, I do.
I often buy …
I never buy …

No, I don't.

14 Write a report. Then say.

Sarah often goes shopping in the supermarket.
She buys fruit, bread and milk.
She never buys fish.

5 Free time

★ **1** 🎧 50 **Listen and point. Then test your partner.**

1. play football
2. play volleyball
3. feed the ducks
4. ride a bike
5. dance
6. cook
7. sail a boat
8. swim
9. skate
10. play the saxophone
11. ski

★ **2 Work in pairs. Mime and guess.**

Play volleyball.

⭐ **3** 51/52 **Listen. Sing the song.**

Busy Lizzy

Her name is Lizzy,
and she's so busy.
She's got so many
things to do.

She feeds the squirrels in the park,
she plays the saxophone.
She rides her bike around the town
and then she dances with a clown.

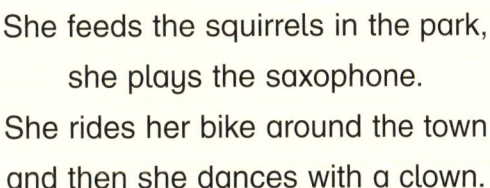

Her name is ...

She goes sailing every day,
and she plays volleyball.
She cooks spaghetti for her friends,
her busy day just never ends.

Her name is ...

🌟 **4 Read and find the mistakes. Say the correct sentences.**

1 Lizzy feeds the ducks in the park.

2 She plays the piano.

3 Lizzy dances with a sheriff.

4 She goes shopping every day.

5 Lizzy plays basketball.

6 She cooks fish and chips for her friends.

Lizzy feeds the ... in the park.

5 Free time

★ **5** 🔊 56 **Listen and remember. Then talk about the children.**

Claire

Robert

Abigail

James

★ **6 Ask a partner.**

A sport for Mr Matt

7 Watch the story and say words you remember. Finish the sentences.

8   Listen and read.

Grace: Hello, Peter.
Peter: Hi, Grace.
Grace: Can I try, please?
Peter: Sure, go ahead.
 …
Grace: It's great!
Peter: You can try again tomorrow.
Grace: Thank you. See you tomorrow.
Peter: Bye.

9 Do a role play.

5 Free time

⭐ **10** Look, read and say.

- Dylan can ride a horse.
- Jake can't skate.
- Brandon can cook.
- Adam can't sail a boat.

Picture number 1 is …

 My text

⭐ **11** Read. Write your own text.

My text
I can cook. I'm good at it.
I can't ski.

⭐⭐ **12** Read. Write your own text.

My text
My best friend is Keira. She is nine. She plays tennis. She is very good at it.
Keira can also ride a horse, but she can't sail a boat.

Hobbies

⭐ **13** Look at the photos. Talk about the children's hobbies.

Who likes …
- metal detecting?
- cooking?
- bird watching?

Bryan's hobby is …

⭐ **14** Watch the video. Who does what?

Bryan   … shows Mia and Mike a cormorant.

　　　　　　　 … often cooks for his family.

Isabel   … sometimes finds things on the beach.

　　　　　　　 … is making chocolate strawberries.

Lucy   … has got a box full of metal things.

　　　　　　　 … loves puffins.

 A poster project: Present your hobby

Bring pictures of your hobbies. Collect English words – ask your teacher for help.

- My hobby is …
- For my hobby I need …
- Every Saturday … / I often …
- I really love my hobby. It's great fun / very interesting.

Presentation tips:
✓ Loud and clear!
✓ Smile.
✓ Point at your picture/photo.

6 Feelings

★ **1** 🔊 1 Listen and point. Then test your partner.

1. sad
2. tired
3. angry
4. scared
5. happy
6. bored
7. nervous

★ **2** Play the memory game.

Tell me about Jeff and Kevin.
That's right.
I think they're angry.
Tell me about Anne.
No, sorry. She's bored.
I think she's nervous.

⭐ **3**  2-4 **Listen. Do the chant.**

Are you happy?

Are you happy?
No, I'm not.

Are you sad?
No, I'm not.

Are you angry?
No, I'm not.

Are you tired?
No, I'm not.

What's the matter?
I'm bored.

⭐ **4** 5 **Listen to the dialogues.**

Dialogue 1:

Nicole: Is he bored?
Charlie: No, he isn't.
Nicole: Is he sad?
Charlie: Yes, he is.
Nicole: What's the matter?
Charlie: His dog is ill.

LOOK!
They're = They are
They aren't = They are not
He/She/It isn't = ... is not

Dialogue 2:

Larry: Are they angry?
Susan: No, they aren't.
Larry: What's the problem?
Susan: They're hungry.

⭐ **5** **Work in pairs. Change the dialogues and act them out.**

6 Feelings

Snow White

⭐ **6** 📺 Watch the story. 🔊 6 Listen and read.

⭐ **7** 🎧 7/8 **Listen. Sing the song.**

Friends

I'm not alone, not alone in the city.
I'm so happy, so happy
I've got friends.

We laugh and shout,
we run around and hop.
We sing and dance,
we never, never stop.

I'm not alone, not alone in the city.
I'm so happy, so happy
I've got friends.

6 Feelings

I'm scared

⭐ **8** Watch the story and say words you remember. Finish the sentences.

⭐ **9** 🎵 10 Listen and read.

Ryan: Help!
Lucy: What is it, Ryan?
Ryan: I'm scared. There's a monster in my bed.
Lucy: Come on, let's check. … Here's your monster. Raaah!
Ryan: Lucy! I'll get you!
Lucy: Good night!

⭐ **10** Do a role play.

38   S. 31

I'm not scared

⭐ **11** 🎵 11 **Listen and point.**

bear   truck   goat   house

log   mat   boat   fly

⭐ **12** 🎵 12 **Listen and say the poem.**

I'm not scared

I'm not scared of
a croc in my sock,
a bee on my knee,
or a bird in my shirt,
but I am scared of
a fly in my eye.

⭐ **13** **Write your own poem and draw a picture.**

a goat on my boat   a rat on my hat   a bear on my chair   a mouse in my house

a bat on my mat   a snake in my cake   a duck in my truck   a frog on a log

7 Time

★ **1** 🎧 13 Listen and point. Test your partner.

1. It's quarter to three.
2. It's half past three.
3. It's quarter past seven.
4. It's six o'clock.
5. It's quarter past one.
6. It's five o'clock.
7. It's quarter to twelve.

★ **2** Ask a partner.

"What's the time on the red clock?"

"It's …"

LOOK!
It's **quarter past** four.
It's **half past** four.
It's **quarter to** five.

⭐ **3** 15-17 **Listen. Do the chant.**

Time for tea

'What's the time?', says Kim.
'It's four o'clock,' says Jim.
'Time for tea,' says Kim.
'Wait for me,' says Jim.

⭐ **4** **Read, look and say the names.**

1 She gets up at seven o'clock. She goes to school at eight o'clock.
She comes home at half past three. She goes to bed at quarter to nine.

2 She gets up at eight o'clock. She goes to school at half past eight.
She comes home at four o'clock. She goes to bed at quarter past nine.

3 She gets up at seven o'clock. She goes to school at quarter to eight.
She comes home at three o'clock. She goes to bed at nine o'clock.

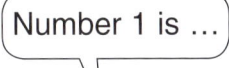

Number 1 is …

7 Time

Going to a party

★ 5 📺 Watch the story and say words you remember. Finish the sentences.

★ 6 🎵 18 **Listen and read.**

Anna: Come on, Jake. It's six o'clock.
Jake: Lots of time to finish the game.
 …
Anna: Jake, it's half past six. We're late!
Jake: Let me finish the game.
Anna: OK, I'm going!
Jake: Wait Anna, I'm coming!

★ 7 Do a role play.

8 Look, read and say.

- Toby comes home at ten past three.
- Harry comes home at quarter to two.
- James comes home at half past three.
- George comes home at twenty to three.

Number one is …

❶  ❷  ❸  ❹

9 Read. Write your own text.

My text

I go to school at half past seven.
I come home at quarter past twelve.

10 Read. Write your own text.

My text

I get up at seven o'clock. I go to school at quarter to eight.
School starts at eight o'clock. I come home at half past twelve.
In the afternoon, I do my homework and play.

7 Time

Midnight on the farm

★ **11** 📺 Watch the story. 🎧 20 **Listen and read.**

Let's keep fit

12 Test your partner. What can she/he do in a minute?

Name	do sit-ups	bend your knees	jump	...
Nick	14	18	16	
Becky	10	15	12	

13 How many times does your heart beat in a minute?

sitting   walking   running

8 At home

★ **1** 🎧 21 Listen and point. Then test your partner.

1. attic
2. wardrobe
3. floor
4. bed
5. bathroom
6. washbasin
7. stairs
8. bedroom
9. kitchen
10. table
11. hall
12. sofa
13. lamp
14. living room

★ **2** Ask a partner.

Where's the rubber?
No, it isn't.
Is it in the kitchen?

46 Poster 8 AB S. 38

3 🔊 22 **Listen and point. Then test your partner.**

under

next to

in

on

in front of

behind

Is the pencil **in** the pencil case?

Is it …?

No, it isn't.

4 Look at the picture in 1. Ask and answer.

Where are Tom's socks?	Where are Kate's trainers?
Where's his cap?	Where's her T-shirt?
Where are his jeans?	Where's her pullover?
Where's his schoolbag?	Where's her umbrella?

Where are Tom's socks?

Where are Kate's trainers?

On the sofa in the living room.

Under the … in the …

8 At home

The hats in the attic

★ 5 📺 Watch the story. 🎧 24 Listen and read.

 6 25/26 **Listen. Sing the song.**

The raccoon in my room

There's a raccoon,
a little raccoon,
a little raccoon
in my room, oh, yes!

He's drinking my milk
and he's eating my bread,
he's breaking my toys
and he's using my bed.

Please, Mum, don't come in.
There's a mess in my room.
I think my raccoon
won't leave before June.

Don't tell anybody
my little raccoon
is just an excuse
for the mess in my room.

8 At home

⭐ **7 Look, read and say.**

- Emma's socks are next to the lamp.
- Ruby's socks are on the lamp.
- Molly's socks are behind the lamp.
- Matilda's socks are under the lamp.

Emma's socks are in picture …

⭐ **8 Read. Write your own text.**

My text

In my room, there's a nice bed.
The desk is in front of the window.
There are three posters in my room.

⭐⭐ **9 Read. Write your own text.**

My text

There are two beds in my room. One for me and one for my sister Olivia. There is no desk, but there are two wardrobes. There are lots of posters in our room. On the posters, there are dogs and cats. My sister likes dogs and I like cats.

Houses and homes

10 Look at the photos and answer the questions.

Which photo shows …
- a semi-detached house?
- a house in the countryside?
- a block of flats?

11  Watch the video. Match the sentences to the pictures above.

- There are lots of cars and it's very noisy here.
- There are lots of shops, cinemas and restaurants nearby.
- It's very quiet here.
- Lots of tourists come here because it is so beautiful.
- It's two houses in one, and they look exactly the same.
- There is a bus stop and a train station near here.
- There are lots of gardens with beautiful flowers.

'It's very quiet here.' is picture number 2.

 A poster project: Crazy houses

Bring pictures of crazy houses. Make a poster.

- This is my crazy house.
- It's a … house.
- It's big/small/…
- It's cool/great.

Presentation tips:
✔ Loud and clear!
✔ Smile.
✔ Point at your picture/photo.

9 Food and drink

⭐ **1** 28 Listen and point. Then test your partner.

1. steak
2. soup
3. sausages
4. beans
5. pie
6. peas
7. lemonade
8. mixed salad
9. tea
10. mineral water
11. coffee
12. chocolate
13. nuts
14. ice cream
15. cake

⭐ **2** Ask your partner.

Do you like …?

Yes, I do. / No, I don't.

3 30/31 **Listen. Sing the song.**

Luba's restaurant

Luba's is a crazy restaurant,
Luba's is the place to go.
Luba's is the place for you and me,
come here and you will see!

There is fish in your orange juice
and ice cream on your steak.
There's fruit on your pizza
and salad on your cake!

Luba's is a crazy restaurant,
Luba's is the place to go.
Luba's is the place for you and me,
come here and you will see!

There are nuts in your tomato soup
and coffee on your pie –
and on top of your dessert
there is a fly!
Oh, no!

4 **Read and say** *True* **or** *False*. **Correct the wrong sentences.**

1. In Luba's restaurant, there is fruit on your cake.
2. There are nuts in your tomato soup.
3. There is salad on your dessert.
4. There is fish in your orange juice.
5. There is chocolate on your steak.
6. There is coffee on your pie.

In Luba's restaurant, there's fruit on your cake.

That's false. In Luba's restaurant, there's fruit on your …

5 **Create a menu for a crazy restaurant.**

9 Food and drink

★ 6 🎵 32 **Listen and read.**

Main courses
chicken | spaghetti
fish | steak
pizza | sausages

Vegetables
beans | chips
peas | potatoes
carrots | mixed salad
spinach

Desserts
apple pie | ice cream
cheesecake | fruit salad
chocolate cake

Drinks
orange juice | lemonade
cola | tea
mineral water

- What would you like to eat?
- Sausages and beans for me, please.
- Fish and chips and a mixed salad, please.
- Fish and chips and a mixed salad. And sausages and beans. And to drink?
- I'm thirsty. A big cola, please.
- An orange juice for me.
- A cola and an orange juice. And for dessert?
- I'd like a fruit salad, please.
- I'd like an ice cream, please.
- Here you are.
- Thanks.

★ 7 **Do a role play.**

54   AB S. 44/2

Toffees for Annabel

8 Watch the story. 36 Listen and read.

9 Food and drink

9 Read and look. Speak.

Tyler likes spaghetti and pizza.
He doesn't like chicken and steak.
He likes orange juice but he doesn't like tea.

Jack likes rice and steak.
He doesn't like mixed salad and hot dogs.
He likes tea but he doesn't like orange juice.

Lilly likes broccoli and fish.
She doesn't like chicken and hot dogs.
She likes tea but she doesn't like coffee.

I think number 1 is …

I think so too. / No, I think it's …

All that food is just for me

★ **10** 🔊 38 **Listen and read the poem.**

Tomato soup,
a muesli bar,
a yoghurt, apples,
chicken, tea.
All that food
is just for me.

Steak and rice,
eggs and cheese,
a cake, an orange,
can't you see?
All that food
is just for me.

How can I put
all that food
in my lunch box
for a start?
Who can help me?
Who's so smart?

★ **11 Write your own poem.**

mixed salad	pie	chocolate	peas	sausages
beans	ice cream	nuts	fish	pizza
chips	spaghetti	spinach	carrots	fruit salad

Special days

Halloween

⭐ **1** 39 **Listen. Say the rhymes.**

Halloween

Halloween, Halloween
scary things can be seen,
witches' hats, coal-black cats,
ghosts and monsters, mice and rats.

Trick or treat!

Witches, ghosts and goblins
running down the street,
knock on every doorway,
'Trick or treat!'

When your door is opened,
this is what you meet,
scary creatures shouting,
'Trick or treat!'

⭐ **2** 40 **Listen and read.**

October 31 is Halloween.

Children in Britain and the USA dress up as witches, ghosts and monsters. There are a lot of Halloween parties. At parties, children play games like apple bobbing. To play apple bobbing, children catch an apple in a bowl of water with their mouths.

Children eat fun food and they make pumpkin lanterns. On the night of Halloween, children go from door to door. They call 'Trick or Treat'. People give them sweets.

Christmas around the world

Special days

★ **1** 🎧 41 **Listen and read.**

"Hi, I'm Ella from Sydney. This is our Christmas."

In Australia, Christmas is in summer, so it's sunny and hot outside.
We have our summer holidays at Christmas.
Many families celebrate Christmas on the beach.
We have a barbecue.
Here is my family on Christmas Day.

Santa Claus comes on a sleigh with six kangaroos.

"Hi, I'm Carter from Calgary."

In Canada, Christmas is in winter, so it is very cold outside. There is a lot of snow.

Here in Calgary, many families like to decorate their houses with lights. This is our house.
In the afternoon, I go on a sleigh ride with Mom and Dad.

59

Special days: Valentine's Day

⭐ **1** 42 **Listen and read.**

February 14 is Valentine's Day. You send a card to someone you love or like very much. But you don't write your name. Children make cards for their mums and dads, their teachers and friends! Some classes decorate their classroom with hearts.

⭐ **2** 43 **Listen to the Valentines poems. Say the poems.**

Roses are red,
violets are blue.
Happy Valentine's Day
from a friend – guess who?

Valentines, valentines
red, white and blue.
I'll make a nice one
and send it to you.

⭐ **3 Make your own Valentine cards.**

①  ②  ⑤

③  ④

⭐⭐ **4 Write cards to three friends.**

60

Pancake Day

Special days

1 44 **Listen and read.**

Pancake Day is 47 days before Easter.
On Pancake Day, many families make pancakes.
They eat the hot pancakes with sugar and lemon juice.
There are many pancake races.
At a pancake race, children run with a pancake in a pan.
When they are running, they toss their pancakes.

2 45-47 **Listen. Do the chant.**

Mix a pancake

Mix a pancake,
stir a pancake,
put it in the pan.
Fry the pancake,
toss the pancake,
catch it if you can.

3 **Make pancakes.**

Pancake Day pancakes
(for 12 small pancakes)

① 100g flour
   Pinch of salt
   2 eggs
② 300 ml milk
③ 50 ml oil
④ Fry the pancake.
   Eat with lemon juice
   and sugar.

Word list: English – German

A
a big hand for …	Applaus für …
above	über
across (the bridge)	über (die Brücke)
act out	nachspielen
afternoon (PW3)	Nachmittag
airport	Flughafen
alone	alleine
angry	wütend
animal (PW3)	Tier
answer	Antwort
anybody	hier: niemand
ask	fragen
attic	Dachboden

B
bag	Tasche
bathroom	Badezimmer
beach	Strand
beans	Bohnen
bear	Bär
the heart beats	das Herz schlägt
beautiful (PW3)	(wunder)schön
bedroom	Schlafzimmer
behind	hinter
bird (PW3)	Vogel
birthday	Geburtstag
black (PW3)	schwarz
block of flats	Wohnblock
boat	Boot
book (PW3)	Buch
bored	gelangweilt
bread	Brot
break	zerbrechen, kaputt machen
bridge	Brücke
bring	bringen
budgie	Wellensittich
busy	hier: (viel)beschäftigt

C
cake	Kuchen
call	(an)rufen
change	hier: verändern
check	überprüfen, kontrollieren
cheese (PW3)	Käse
chewing gum	Kaugummi
chocolate	Schokolade
cinema	Kino
city	Stadt, Großstadt
clean	sauber
clear	klar, deutlich
clock	Uhr
clothes (PW3)	Kleidung
colour (PW3)	Farbe; anmalen
cormorant	hier: Kormoran
come home	heimkommen
cook	kochen
count	zählen
in the countryside	auf dem Land
crazy (PW3)	verrückt

D
play darts	Dart spielen, mit Wurfpfeilen spielen
December	Dezember
dessert	Nachspeise
down	hinunter
draw (PW3)	zeichnen
drink (PW3)	trinken
drinks	hier: Getränke
duck (PW3)	Ente

E
ear (PW3)	Ohr
easy	leicht
eighty	achtzig
exactly	genau
Excuse me.	Entschuldigung.
eye (PW3)	Auge

F
face (PW3)	Gesicht
false (PW3)	falsch
fantastic (PW3)	fantastisch
feed the ducks	Enten füttern
fifty	fünfzig
find	finden
fire brigade	Feuerwehr
fist	Faust
fit	hier: passen
floor	Boden
flower (PW3)	Blume
fly (PW3)	fliegen, Fliege
food (PW3)	Speisen, Essen
foot/feet (PW3)	Fuß/Füße
forty	vierzig
Friday (PW3)	Freitag
friend (PW3)	Freund/in
frog (PW3)	Frosch
fruit	Früchte, Obst

G
get up (PW3)	aufstehen
I will get you!	Ich kriege dich! Ich erwische dich!
go (PW3)	gehen
go away	weggehen

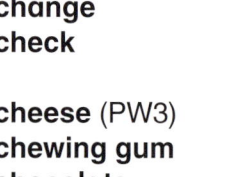

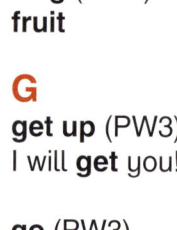

Word list

go to bed	schlafen gehen	**M**	
go to school	zur Schule gehen	main course	Hauptspeise
goat	Ziege	March	März
grab	zupacken, greifen	marry	heiraten
guess	raten	mat	(Fuß) Matte
guinea pig 	Meerschweinchen	match	zuordnen
		Maths	Mathematik, Rechnen
H		do Maths	rechnen üben
It's **half past** one.	Es ist **halb** zwei.	What's the **matter**?	Was ist los?
hall	Hausflur	**May**	Mai
hat (PW3)	Hut	mess	Unordnung, Durcheinander
hate (PW3)	hassen		
have (PW3)	haben	midnight	Mitternacht
hear (PW3)	hören	(glass of) **milk** (PW3)	(Glas) Milch
heart	Herz	mineral water	Mineralwasser
help (PW3)	helfen	mixed salad 	gemischter Salat
homework	Hausübung	**Monday** (PW3)	Montag
hospital	Krankenhaus	money	Geld
house (PW3)	Haus	month	Monat
come to my **house**	komm zu mir **nach** Hause	mouse/mice	Maus/Mäuse
(a) hundred	hundert	**N**	
hungry (PW3)	hungrig	nearby	in der Nähe
hurry up	sich beeilen	nervous	nervös
		next to	neben
I		ninety	neunzig
ice cream 	Eis	nuts	Nüsse
idea (PW3)	Idee		
ill (PW3) 	krank	**O**	
in front of	vor	It is one **o'clock**.	Es ist ein **Uhr**.
invitation	Einladung	on	auf
iron	hier: bügeln	opposite	gegenüber
J		**P**	
join in 	mitmachen	It's ten **past** one.	Es ist zehn **nach** eins.
July	Juli	**peas** (PW3)	Erbsen
June	Juni	pence	Pennies (engl. Währung)
		pet	Haustier
K		pick	pflücken
king (PW3)	König	picture	Bild
kitchen 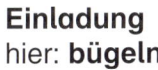	Küche	pie	Kuchen
knee (PW3)	Knie	piggy bank	Sparschwein
		playground	Spielplatz
L		poem	Gedicht
lamp	Lampe	**point** (PW3) 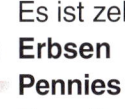	zeigen (auf)
late	spät	post office	Postamt
left (PW3)	links	potato	Kartoffel
lemonade 	Limonade	pound	Pfund (engl. Währung)
library	Bücherei, Bibliothek	**present** (PW3)	Geschenk
living room	Wohnzimmer	puffin	Papageientaucher
log	Holzklotz	pull	ziehen
look (PW3)	schauen		
loud	laut		
lovely	nett, reizend		
lunch box (PW3) 	Pausenbrotdose		

63

Word list: English – German

put on (PW3)	anziehen

Q
quarter (past/to)	viertel (nach/vor)
queen	Königin
question	Frage
quiet (PW3)	leise, ruhig

R
rabbit (PW3)	Kaninchen, Hase
rat (PW3)	Ratte
raven	Rabe
remember	sich erinnern
ride a bike	Rad fahren
right (PW3)	rechts, richtig
river (PW3)	Fluss
room	Zimmer
run	laufen

S
sad (PW3)	traurig
sail (a boat)	segeln
same	gleich
Saturday (PW3)	Samstag
sausages	Würstchen
say (PW3) 	sagen
scared	ängstlich, verängstigt
school (PW3)	Schule
scissors (PW3)	Schere
sentence	Satz
seventy	siebzig
shirt	Hemd
shopping list	Einkaufsliste
sightseeing	Sehenswürdigkeiten besichtigen
silly	dumm
sixty	sechzig
skate	Schlittschuh laufen, inlineskaten
ski	Ski laufen
sleep (PW3)	schlafen
smart	klug
smile	lächeln
soup	Suppe
speak (PW3)	sprechen
spider	Spinne
spinach	Spinat
squirrel	Eichhörnchen
stairs	Treppe, Treppenhaus
steak	Steak
story	Geschichte
straight on 	geradeaus
strawberry	Erdbeere
stupid	dumm
Sunday (PW3)	Sonntag

survey	Umfrage
sweet shop 	Süßigkeitenladen
sweets	Süßigkeiten

T
table	Tisch
take (PW3)	nehmen
tea (PW3)	Tee
tooth/teeth (PW3)	Zahn/Zähne
things	Dinge, Sachen
thirty	dreißig
Thursday (PW3)	Donnerstag
tickle	kitzeln
time	Zeit
tired	müde
It's ten to one.	Es ist zehn vor eins.
today	heute
toffees	Karamellbonbon
tomorrow	morgen
tortoise	Schildkröte
town	Stadt, Kleinstadt
train station	Bahnhof
tree (PW3)	Baum
truck	Lastwagen
true (PW3)	richtig
try on (PW3)	anprobieren
Tuesday (PW3)	Dienstag
turn right/left	nach rechts/links abbiegen
twenty	zwanzig

U
under	unter
use	benutzen

V
vegetable (PW3)	Gemüse

W
wait	warten
wake up (PW3)	aufwachen
walk	zu Fuß gehen
wardrobe	Kleiderschrank
washbasin	Waschbecken
watch	Armbanduhr
Wednesday (PW3)	Mittwoch
Where?	Wo?
word	Wort
work	arbeiten
write (PW3)	schreiben
wrong	falsch

Y
year (PW3)	Jahr